Cryptocurrency has emerged as a disruptive force in the financial world, offering a decentralized, secure, and efficient alternative to traditional banking systems. However, the safety of cryptocurrencies remains a primary concern for their mainstream adoption. In this book, we will explore the safety aspects of cryptocurrencies, analyzing potential risks and the security measures in place to address them.

Understanding Cryptocurrency Safety

Cryptocurrency safety encompasses various elements, including the protection of digital assets, the integrity of transactions, and the security of user information. For mainstream adoption to occur, individuals and institutions must have confidence in the safety and security of cryptocurrencies. Let us delve into the risks associated with cryptocurrencies and the measures taken to mitigate them.

Risks Associated with Cryptocurrencies - Market Volatility

Cryptocurrencies are known for their price volatility, which can lead to significant financial gains or losses. Market speculation, regulatory changes, and macroeconomic factors can all contribute to price fluctuations. While volatility presents investment opportunities, it also poses risks for mainstream adoption, as stability is crucial for everyday financial transactions.

Cybersecurity Threats

Despite the advanced security measures implemented in the cryptocurrency ecosystem, cyber threats remain a concern. Hacking incidents, phishing attacks, and malware targeting wallets and exchanges have occurred, resulting in substantial losses for individuals and organizations. Cybercriminals continually evolve their techniques, requiring constant vigilance and improved security protocols.

Regulatory and Legal Uncertainties

The regulatory landscape surrounding cryptocurrencies varies across jurisdictions, with some countries embracing them while others impose restrictions or remain uncertain. Inconsistent regulations can create legal complexities, investor uncertainty, and potential risks for mainstream adoption. Clear and coherent regulatory frameworks are essential to establish trust and ensure a level playing field for participants.

Scams, Fraud, and Ponzi Schemes

The decentralized nature of cryptocurrencies, coupled with the pseudonymous identities of users, has attracted fraudulent actors seeking to exploit unsuspecting individuals. Scams and fraudulent schemes, including Ponzi schemes and initial coin offering (ICO) fraud, have been prevalent. Robust investor education, increased regulatory oversight, and industry self-regulation are necessary to mitigate these risks.

Lack of Consumer Protection Mechanisms

Unlike traditional financial systems, cryptocurrencies often lack the same level of consumer protection mechanisms, such as insurance on digital assets or dispute resolution mechanisms. In the event of a hack, loss, or fraudulent activity, recovering lost funds can be challenging, and the burden of security often rests on individual users. Building trust through enhanced consumer protection measures is crucial for mainstream adoption.

Security Measures in the Cryptocurrency Ecosystem - Blockchain Technology

The underlying technology of most cryptocurrencies, blockchain, provides a decentralized and transparent ledger system. Transactions recorded on the blockchain are immutable and cannot be easily altered, ensuring the integrity of the cryptocurrency ecosystem. The distributed nature of blockchain reduces the risk of a single point of failure and enhances security.

Cryptographic Techniques

Cryptocurrencies employ robust cryptographic techniques to secure transactions and protect user privacy. Public-key cryptography enables secure communication and authentication between participants. Hashing algorithms ensure the integrity of the blockchain by making it computationally infeasible to alter previous transactions. These cryptographic measures form the foundation of secure cryptocurrency transactions.

Wallet Security

  Cryptocurrency wallets, whether software, hardware, or online-based, play a crucial role in storing and managing digital assets. Users are advised to choose reputable wallet providers and employ strong passwords, two-factor authentication (2FA), and biometric authentication methods to enhance wallet security. Cold storage wallets, which keep private keys offline, provide an additional layer of protection against online attacks.

Exchange and Platform Security

Cryptocurrency exchanges and platforms have implemented various security measures to protect user funds and data. These include multi-signature wallets, withdrawal limits, real-time monitoring for suspicious activities, and encryption of user information. Reputable exchanges also undergo regular security audits to identify vulnerabilities and improve their overall security posture.

Education and Awareness

Increasing user education and awareness about best practices and potential risks are essential for cryptocurrency safety. Educational resources, tutorials, and community-driven initiatives can empower individuals to make informed decisions and take necessary security precautions. Additionally, promoting responsible use, caution against scams, and adherence to security protocols will contribute to a safer cryptocurrency ecosystem.

Conclusion

The safety of cryptocurrencies is a crucial factor for their mainstream adoption. While risks exist, various security measures have been implemented to address them. Blockchain technology provides a decentralized and transparent framework, cryptographic techniques ensure secure transactions, and wallet security and platform measures protect digital assets. Furthermore, increased regulatory clarity, improved consumer protection mechanisms, and education can further enhance safety in the cryptocurrency ecosystem.

As the industry continues to evolve, it is essential to stay vigilant and adopt best practices for security. Collaboration between industry participants, regulatory authorities, and users is necessary to foster a safe environment for the mainstream adoption of cryptocurrencies. With continuous innovation, effective risk mitigation strategies, and user empowerment, the safety of cryptocurrencies can be enhanced, paving the way for their widespread acceptance in the future.

Below we have provided space for notation:

_____

_____

_____

_____

_____

_____

_____

_____

_____

_____

_____

_____